Honey Badgers

by Margo Gates

BELLWETHER MEDIA • MINNEAPOLIS, MN

Note to Librarians, Teachers, and Parents:

Blastoff! Readers are carefully developed by literacy experts and combine standards-based content with developmentally appropriate text.

Level 1 provides the most support through repetition of high-frequency words, light text, predictable sentence patterns, and strong visual support.

Level 2 offers early readers a bit more challenge through varied simple sentences, increased text load, and less repetition of high-frequency words.

Level 3 advances early-fluent readers toward fluency through increased text and concept load, less reliance on visuals, longer sentences, and more literary language.

Level 4 builds reading stamina by providing more text per page, increased use of punctuation, greater variation in sentence patterns, and increasingly challenging vocabulary.

Level 5 encourages children to move from "learning to read" to "reading to learn" by providing even more text, varied writing styles, and less familiar topics.

Whichever book is right for your reader, Blastoff! Readers are the perfect books to build confidence and encourage a love of reading that will last a lifetime!

This edition first published in 2014 by Bellwether Media, Inc.

No part of this publication may be reproduced in whole or in part without written permission of the publisher. For information regarding permission, write to Bellwether Media, Inc., Attention: Permissions Department, 5357 Penn Avenue South, Minneapolis, MN 55419.

Library of Congress Cataloging-in-Publication Data

Gates, Margo.
Honey badgers / by Margo Gates.
    p. cm. – (Blastoff! readers. Animal safari)
  Summary: "Developed by literacy experts for students in kindergarten through grade three, this book introduces honey badgers to young readers through leveled text and related photos"– Provided by publisher.
  Audience: K to grade 3.
  Includes bibliographical references and index.
  ISBN 978-1-60014-909-2 (hardcover : alk. paper)
  1. Honey badger–Juvenile literature. I. Title. II. Series: Blastoff! readers. 1, Animal safari.
  QL737.C25G3848 2014
  599.76'62–dc23
                                                                      2013000881

Contents

What Are Honey Badgers?

Honey badgers are small **mammals**. They have flat bodies and short legs.

Honey badgers
live in forests and
dry grasslands.

They sleep in **burrows** during the day. They also rest under rocks and tree **roots**.

Hunting for Food

Honey badgers hunt for food at night. They walk slowly and sniff the ground.

They smell mice
and lizards
underground.
Strong legs help
them dig up
their **prey**.

Honey badgers break open beehives with sharp **claws**. They feast on honey and **grubs**.

beehive

Honey badgers also hunt snakes. Thick skin protects them from bites.

Staying Safe

Honey badgers can give off a strong smell. Their stink keeps other animals away.

Honey badgers like to pick fights. They even stand up to lions and wild dogs!

Glossary

burrows—holes or tunnels that some animals dig in the ground

claws—sharp, curved nails at the end of an animal's fingers and toes

grubs—very young bees

mammals—warm-blooded animals that have backbones and feed their young milk

prey—animals that are hunted by other animals for food

roots—the parts of plants that grow into the ground

To Learn More

AT THE LIBRARY

Odone, Jamison. *Honey Badgers*. Asheville, N.C.: Front Street, 2007.

Quinlan, Julia J. *Honey Badgers*. New York, N.Y.: PowerKids Press, 2013.

Sayre, April Pulley. *If You Should Hear A Honey Guide*. Boston, Mass.: Houghton Mifflin, 1995.

ON THE WEB

Learning more about honey badgers is as easy as 1, 2, 3.

1. Go to www.factsurfer.com.

2. Enter "honey badgers" into the search box.

3. Click the "Surf" button and you will see a list of related Web sites.

With factsurfer.com, finding more information is just a click away.

Index

The images in this book are reproduced through the courtesy of: Camptoloma, front cover, p. 5; Minden Pictures/ SuperStock, pp. 7, 21; Nadiia Gerbish, p. 7 (left); ODM, p. 7 (right); Phillip Perry/ FLPA/Newscom, p. 9; Pete Oxford/ Nature Picture Library, p. 11; Yossi Eshbol/ FLPA, p. 13; CreativeNature.nl, p. 13 (left); PhotoSky, p. 13 (right); Marius Becker/ Newscom, p. 15; Debbie Steinhausser, p. 15 (small); Des and Jen Bartlett/ National Geographic Stock, p. 17; Eliot Lyons/ Nature Picture Library, p. 19.